# STEP-BY-STEP

# Drawing Dinosaurs

There are also some other creatures to draw that
were alive at the same time as the dinosaurs.

DESIGNED AND ILLUSTRATED BY
Candice Whatmore

WRITTEN BY
Fiona Watt

# How to draw a Tyrannosaurus rex (tie-ran-oh-sore-us rex)

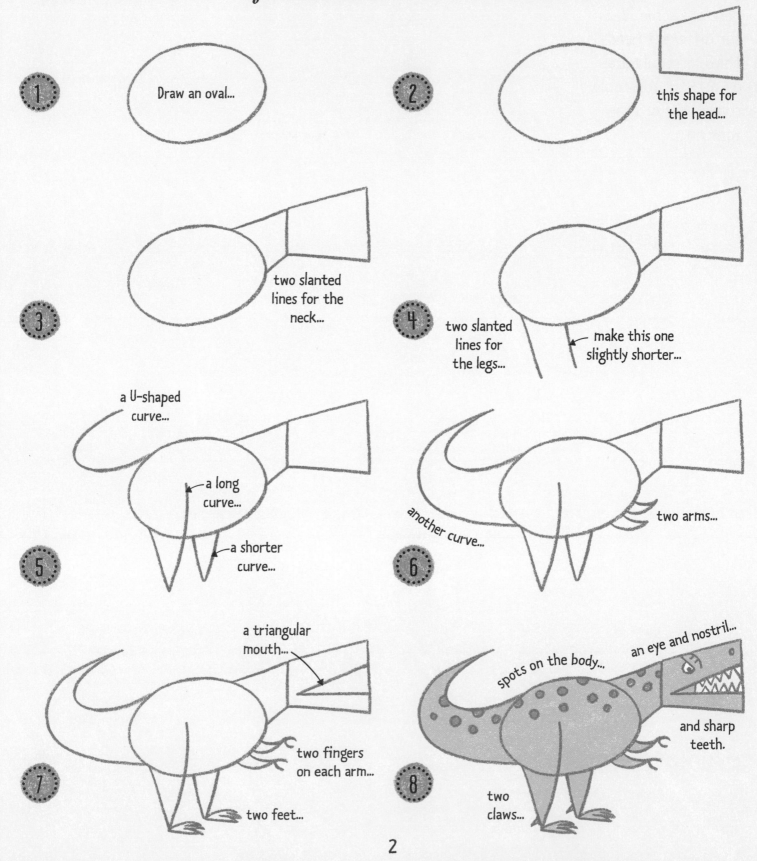

**1** Draw an oval...

**2** this shape for the head...

**3** two slanted lines for the neck...

**4** two slanted lines for the legs... make this one slightly shorter...

**5** a U-shaped curve... a long curve... a shorter curve...

**6** another curve... two arms...

**7** a triangular mouth... two fingers on each arm... two feet...

**8** spots on the body... an eye and nostril... and sharp teeth. two claws...

2

# Try this...

Here are some ideas for different heads that you could draw on a T-rex. You could copy these or draw your own.

curious

roooaaaaarrr!

sleepy

# Your turn...

# How to draw a Sauropelta
### (sore-oh-pel-tah)

Your turn...

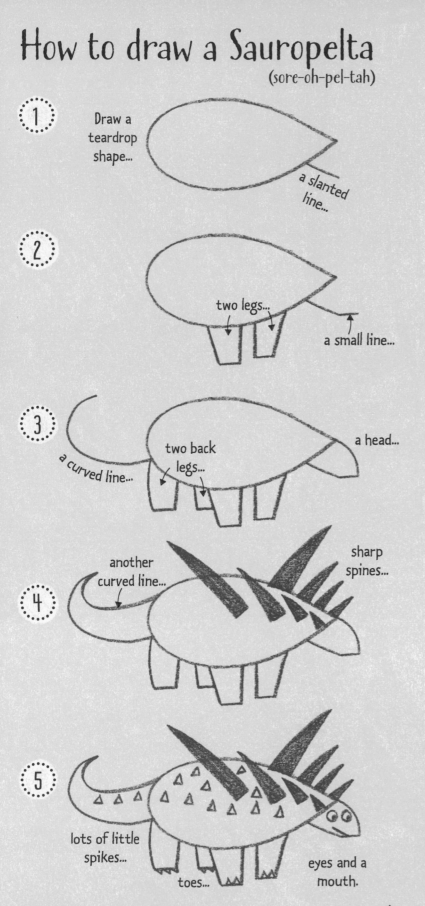

1. Draw a teardrop shape... a slanted line...

2. two legs... a small line...

3. a curved line... two back legs... a head...

4. another curved line... sharp spines...

5. lots of little spikes... toes... eyes and a mouth.

4

# How to draw a Protoceratops (pro-toe-sera-tops)

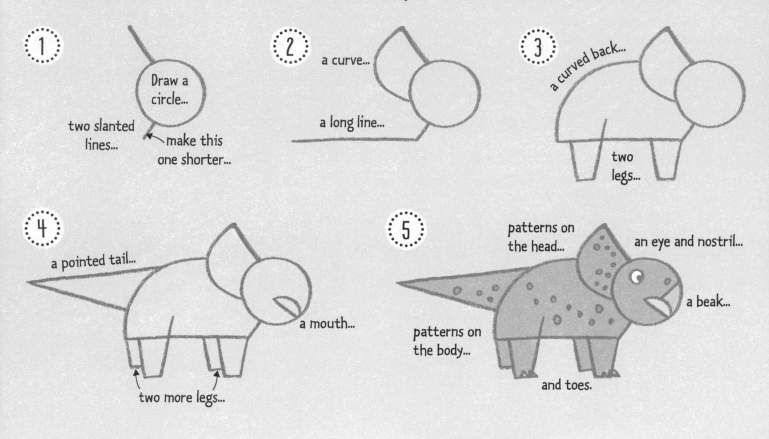

① Draw a circle...

two slanted lines...

make this one shorter...

② a curve...

a long line...

③ a curved back...

two legs...

④ a pointed tail...

a mouth...

two more legs...

⑤ patterns on the head...

an eye and nostril...

a beak...

patterns on the body...

and toes.

Your turn...

# How to draw a Gnathosaurus (nath-oh-sore-us)

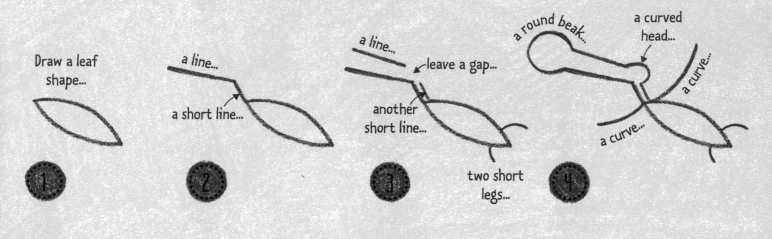

Draw a leaf shape...

**1**

a line...

a short line...

**2**

a line...

leave a gap...

another short line...

two short legs...

**3**

a round beak...

a curved head...

a curve...

a curve...

**4**

Your turn...

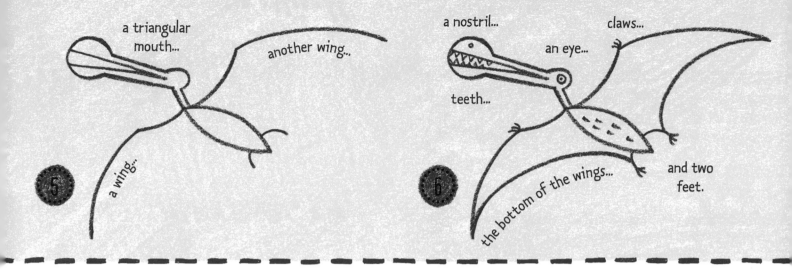

a triangular mouth...

another wing..

a wing...

**5**

a nostril...

claws...

an eye...

teeth...

the bottom of the wings...

and two feet.

**6**

Try drawing a Gnathosaurus flying like this.

# How to draw an Argentinosaurus (ar-jen-teen-oh-sore-us)

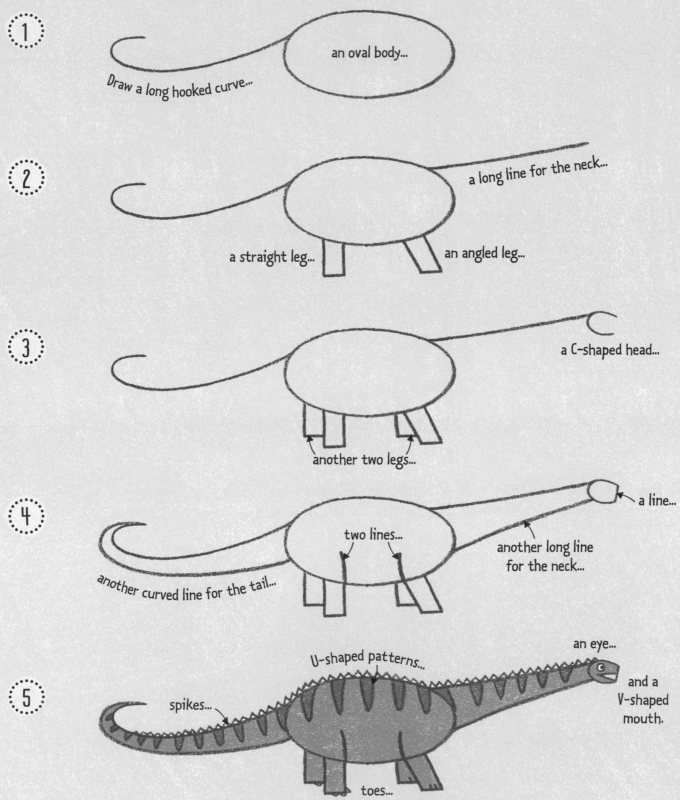

1. Draw a long hooked curve... an oval body...

2. a long line for the neck... a straight leg... an angled leg...

3. a C-shaped head... another two legs...

4. two lines... a line... another long line for the neck... another curved line for the tail...

5. U-shaped patterns... an eye... spikes... and a V-shaped mouth. toes...

Your turn...

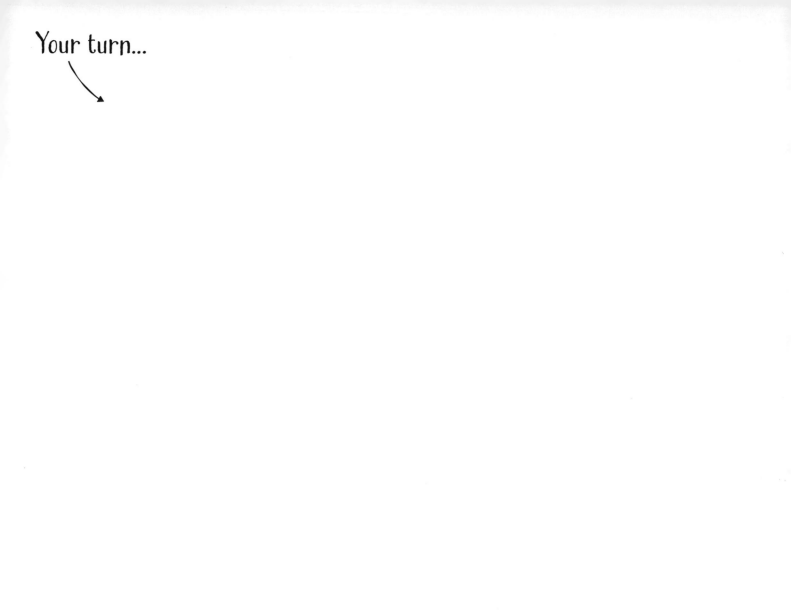

# How to draw a Dimetrodon
(die-met-roe-don)

Your turn...

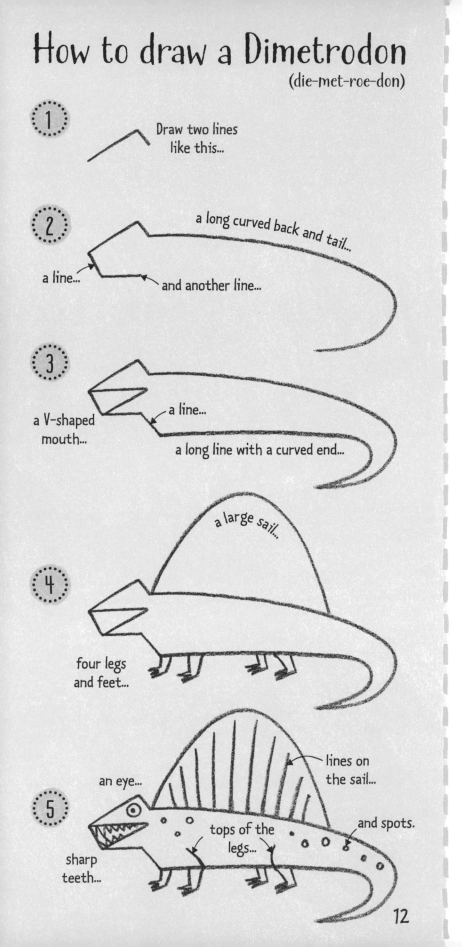

**1** Draw two lines like this...

**2** a long curved back and tail...
a line... and another line...

**3** a V-shaped mouth...
a line...
a long line with a curved end...

**4** a large sail...
four legs and feet...

**5** an eye...
lines on the sail...
sharp teeth...
tops of the legs...
and spots.

12

# How to draw a Shonisaurus (show-nee-sore-us)

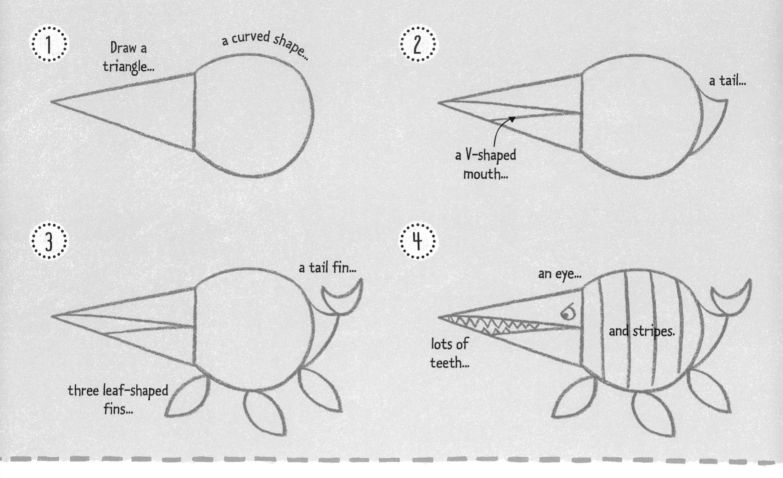

① Draw a triangle... a curved shape...

② a V-shaped mouth... a tail...

③ a tail fin... three leaf-shaped fins...

④ an eye... lots of teeth... and stripes.

Your turn...

Shonisaurus ate
squid like these.

# How to draw a Iguanodon
(ig-wah-noh-don)

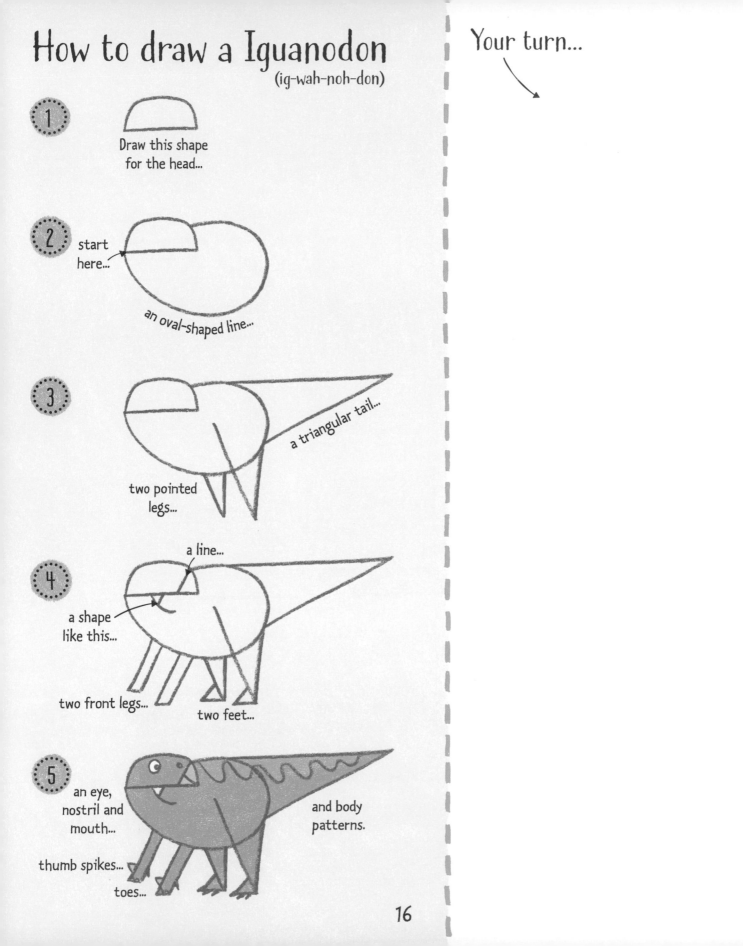

**1** Draw this shape for the head...

**2** start here... an oval-shaped line...

**3** a triangular tail... two pointed legs...

**4** a line... a shape like this... two front legs... two feet...

**5** an eye, nostril and mouth... thumb spikes... toes... and body patterns.

16

# How to draw a Therizinosaurus (thair-i-zin-oh-sore-us)

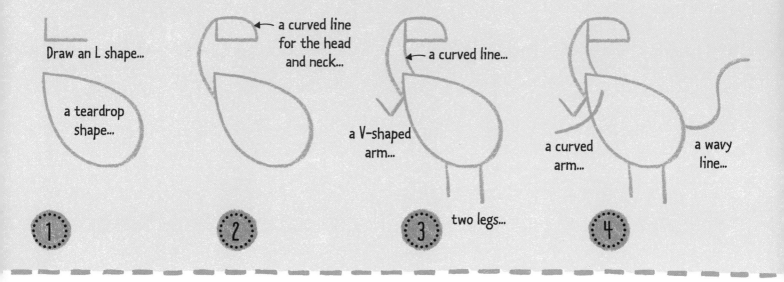

Draw an L shape...

a teardrop shape...

a curved line for the head and neck...

a curved line...

a V-shaped arm...

two legs...

a curved arm...

a wavy line...

**1**

**2**

**3**

**4**

Your turn...

three huge claws
on each arm...

a wavy
tail...

**5** two curved lines
for the legs...

a wing...

a wing...

**6** two feet...

feathers on
the neck...

an eye, nostril
and mouth...

feathers on
the body...

and feathers
on the tail.

**7** Fill in the claws.

19

# How to draw a Citipati
(chit-ee-puh-tee)

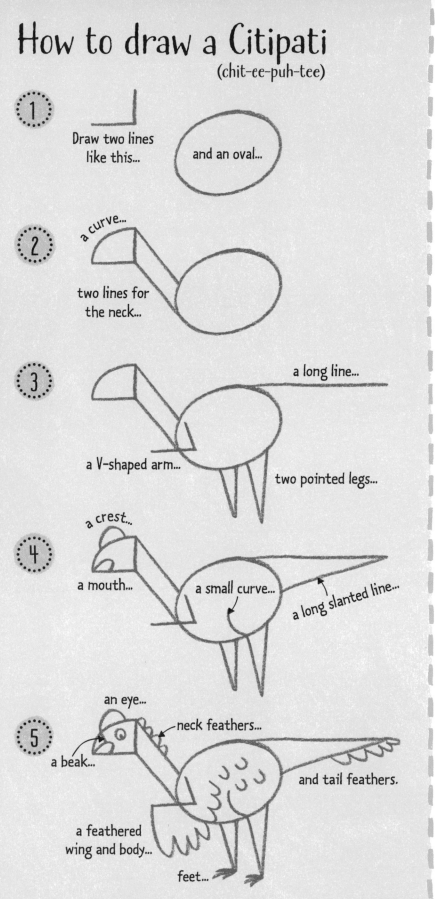

1 Draw two lines like this...

and an oval...

2 a curve...

two lines for the neck...

3 a long line...

a V-shaped arm...

two pointed legs...

4 a crest...

a mouth...

a small curve...

a long slanted line...

5 an eye...

neck feathers...

a beak...

and tail feathers.

a feathered wing and body...

feet...

20

# How to draw a Spinosaurus (spy-no-sore-us)

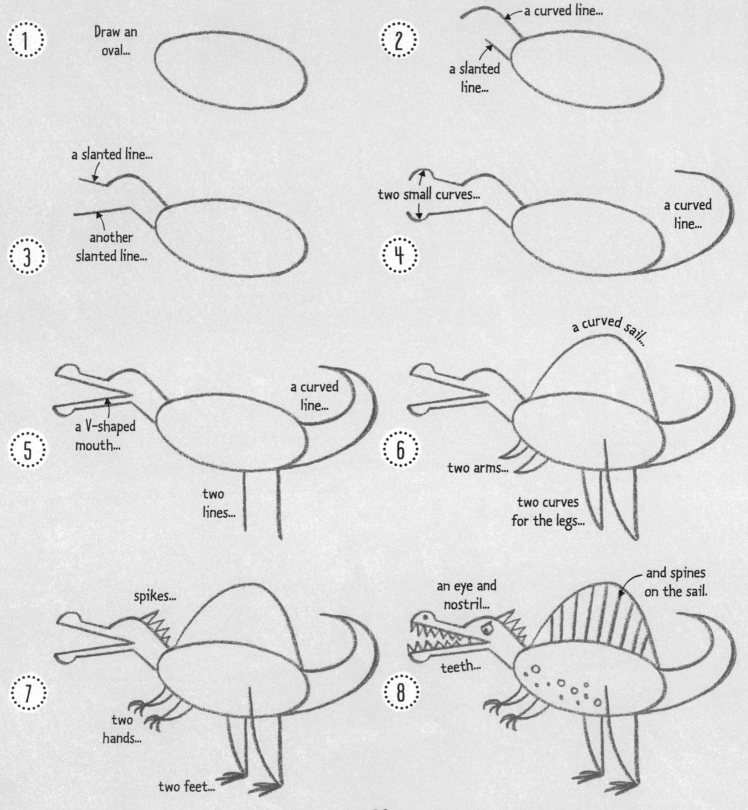

1. Draw an oval...

2. a curved line...
   a slanted line...

3. a slanted line...
   another slanted line...

4. two small curves...
   a curved line...

5. a V-shaped mouth...
   a curved line...
   two lines...

6. a curved sail...
   two arms...
   two curves for the legs...

7. spikes...
   two hands...
   two feet...

8. an eye and nostril...
   teeth...
   and spines on the sail.

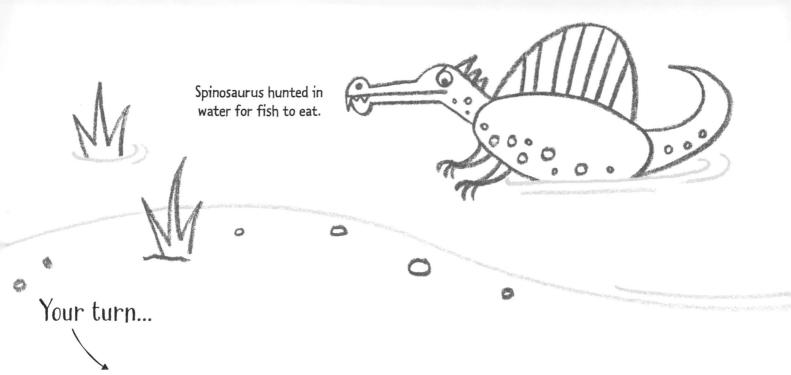

Spinosaurus hunted in water for fish to eat.

Your turn...

# How to draw a Minmi (min-mee)

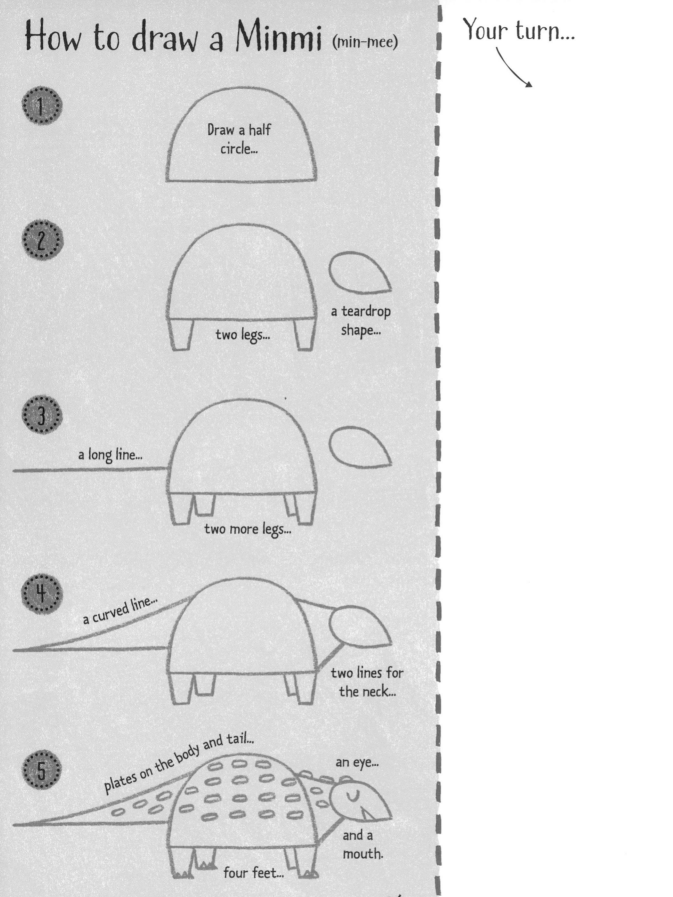

**1** Draw a half circle...

**2** two legs...
a teardrop shape...

**3** a long line...
two more legs...

**4** a curved line...
two lines for the neck...

**5** plates on the body and tail...
an eye...
and a mouth.
four feet...

Your turn...

# How to draw a Pterodactylus
(ter-oh-dak-til-us)

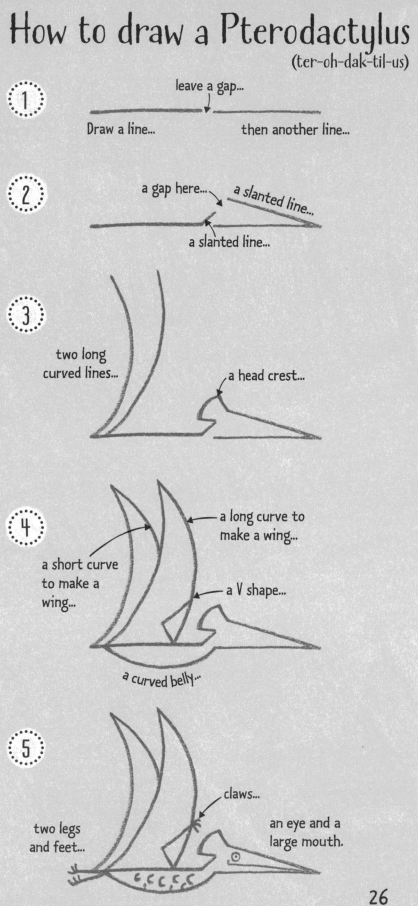

**1** leave a gap...

Draw a line... then another line...

**2** a gap here... a slanted line...

a slanted line...

**3** two long curved lines...

a head crest...

**4** a long curve to make a wing...

a short curve to make a wing...

a V shape...

a curved belly...

**5** claws...

two legs and feet...

an eye and a large mouth.

26

# Try this...

To draw a Pterodactylus flying like this, draw the body and wings of the Gnathosaurus on page 8-9, then add the head and beak of a Pterodactylus.

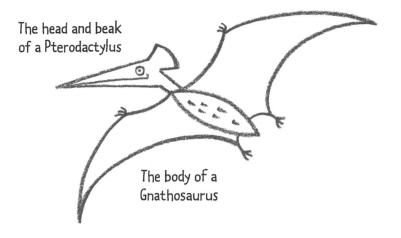

The head and beak of a Pterodactylus

The body of a Gnathosaurus

# How to draw a Styracosaurus (sty-rack-uh-sore-us)

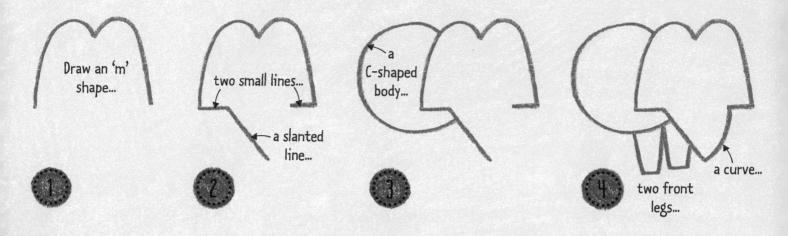

Draw an 'm' shape...

**1**

two small lines...

a slanted line...

**2**

a C-shaped body...

**3**

two front legs...

a curve...

**4**

Your turn...

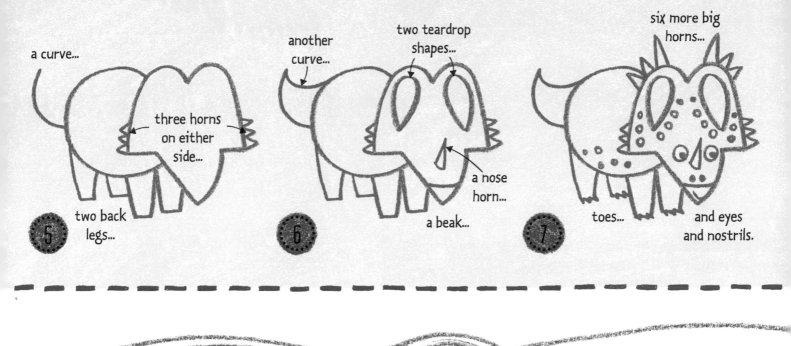

a curve...

three horns on either side...

**5** two back legs...

another curve...

two teardrop shapes...

a nose horn...

**6** a beak...

six more big horns...

**7** toes...

and eyes and nostrils.

# How to draw a Diplodocus (dip-lod-oh-kus)

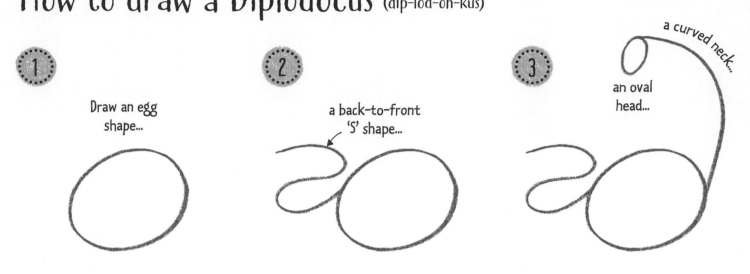

**1** Draw an egg shape...

**2** a back-to-front 'S' shape...

**3** an oval head...

a curved neck...

- - - - - - - - - - - - - - - - - - - - - - -

Your turn...

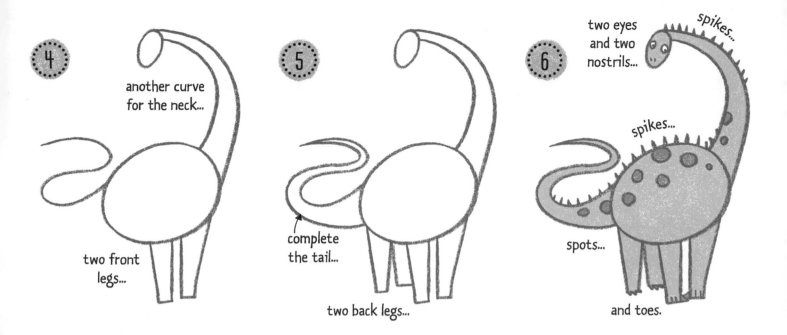

**4** another curve for the neck...

two front legs...

**5** complete the tail...

two back legs...

**6** two eyes and two nostrils...

spikes...

spikes...

spots...

and toes.

# How to draw a Coelophysis (see-loh-fie-sis)

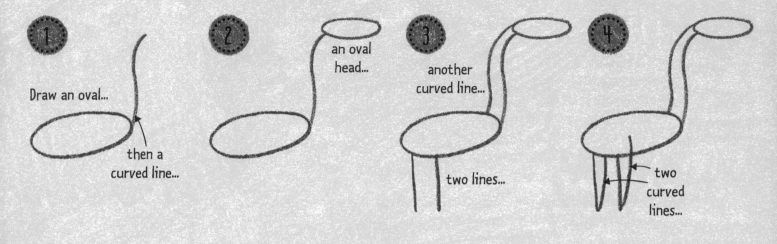

1 Draw an oval... then a curved line...

2 an oval head...

3 another curved line... two lines...

4 two curved lines...

Your turn...

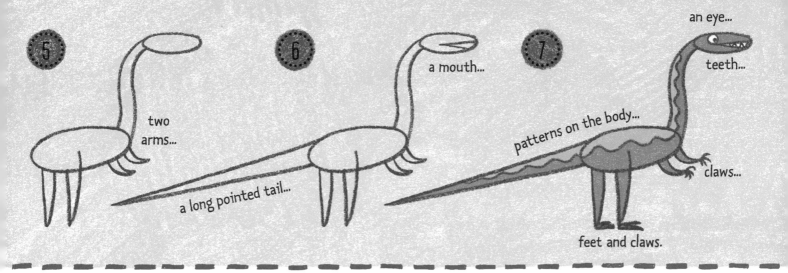

5 two arms...

a long pointed tail...

6 a mouth...

7 patterns on the body...

an eye...

teeth...

claws...

feet and claws.

# How to draw a Rhomaleosaurus (row-mail-lee-oh-sore-us)

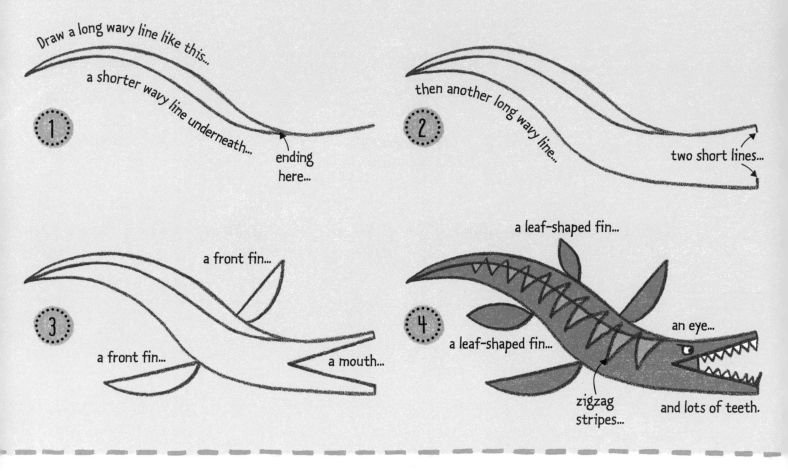

Draw a long wavy line like this...

a shorter wavy line underneath...

ending here...

**1**

then another long wavy line...

two short lines...

**2**

a front fin...

**3**

a front fin...

a mouth...

a leaf-shaped fin...

**4**

a leaf-shaped fin...

an eye...

zigzag stripes...

and lots of teeth.

Your turn...

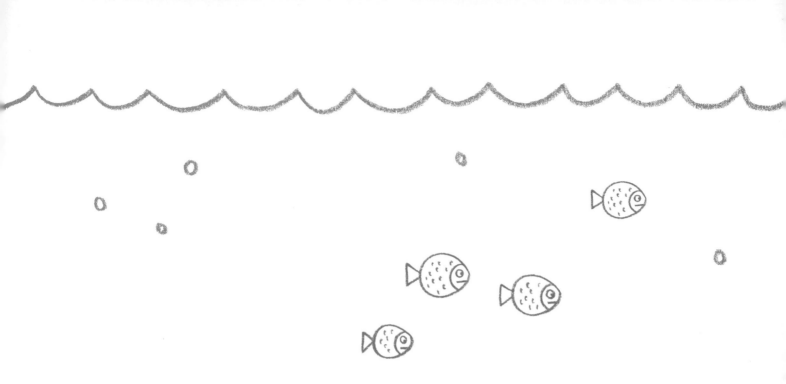

# How to draw an Incisivosaurus

(in-size-see-voh-sore-us)

Your turn...

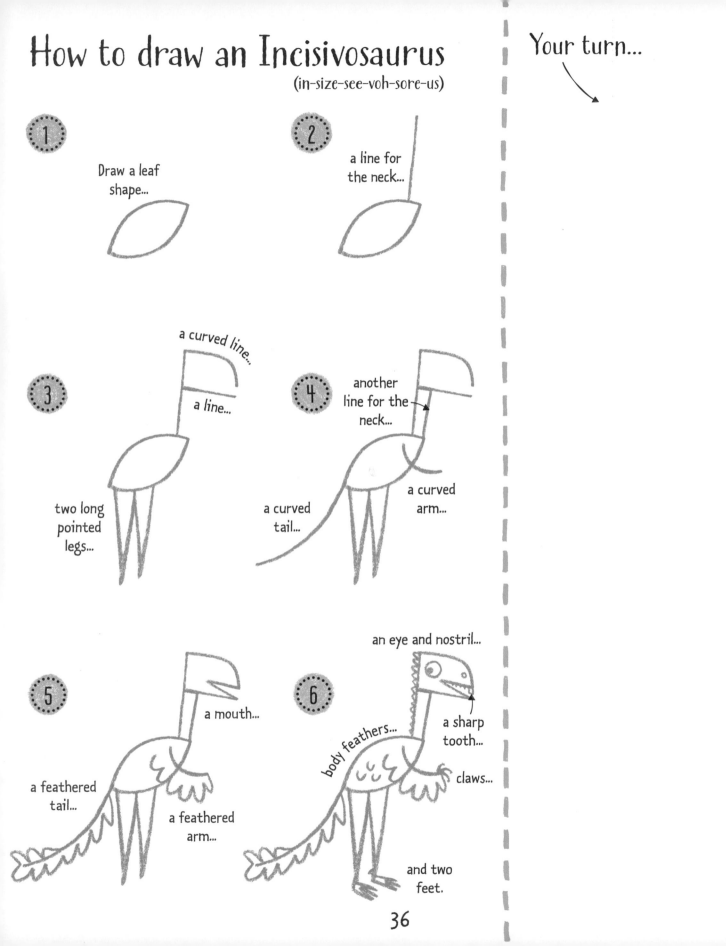

**1** Draw a leaf shape...

**2** a line for the neck...

**3** a curved line... a line... two long pointed legs...

**4** another line for the neck... a curved arm... a curved tail...

**5** a mouth... a feathered tail... a feathered arm...

**6** an eye and nostril... a sharp tooth... claws... body feathers... and two feet.

# How to draw a Dilophosaurus (dye-loh-fuh-sore-us)

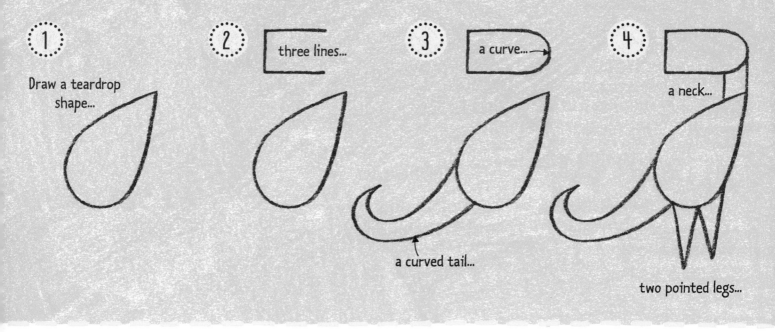

① Draw a teardrop shape...

② three lines...

③ a curve... → a curved tail...

④ a neck... two pointed legs...

Your turn...

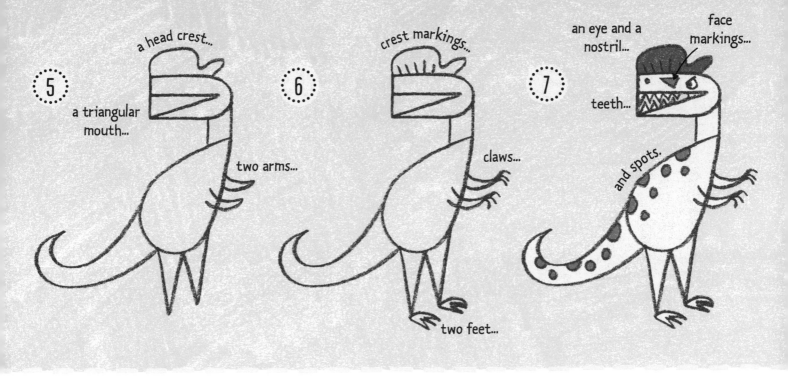

**5** a head crest...

a triangular mouth...

two arms...

**6** crest markings...

claws...

two feet...

**7** an eye and a nostril...

face markings...

teeth...

and spots.

# How to draw a Maiasaura (my-yah-sore-ah)

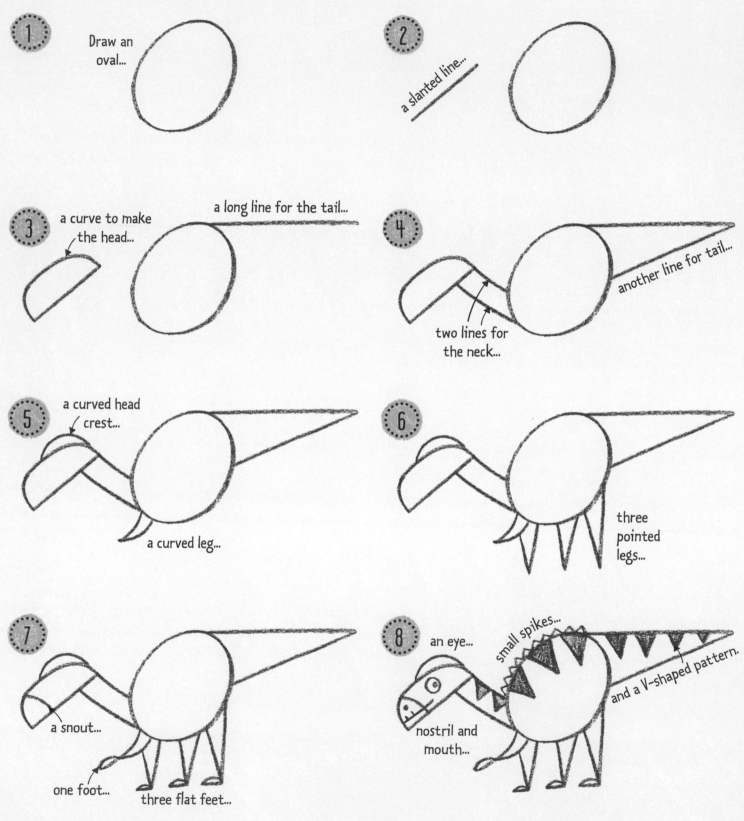

**1** Draw an oval...

**2** a slanted line...

**3** a curve to make the head... a long line for the tail...

**4** two lines for the neck... another line for tail...

**5** a curved head crest... a curved leg...

**6** three pointed legs...

**7** a snout... one foot... three flat feet...

**8** an eye... small spikes... nostril and mouth... and a V-shaped pattern.

Your turn...

# How to draw a Dacentrurus

(day-sen-troo-rus)

**1** Draw this shape for the body...

**2** start here... a long curved line...

a leaf shape...

**3** another curved line...

two legs...

**4** thick spikes... some thinner spikes...

a nose line...

two more legs...

**5** and zigzag stripes.

an eye, nostril and mouth... toes...

Your turn...

42

# How to draw a Quetzalcoatlus (kwet-sal-koh-at-lus)

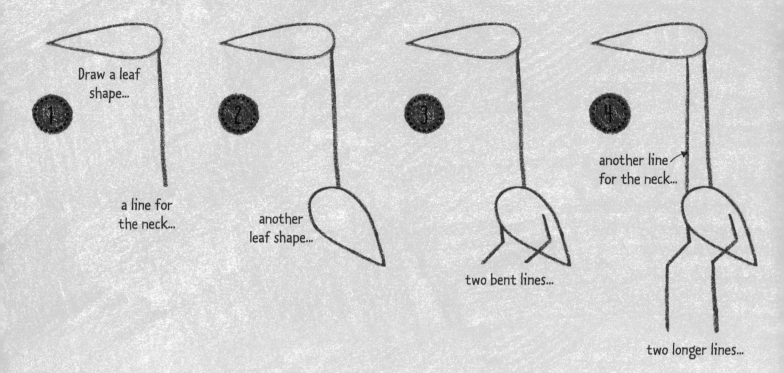

**1** Draw a leaf shape...

a line for the neck...

**2** another leaf shape...

**3** two bent lines...

**4** another line for the neck...

two longer lines...

Your turn...

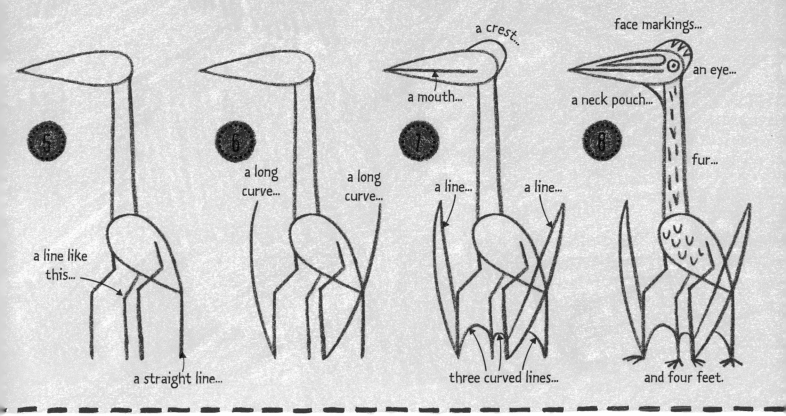

**5**

a line like this...

a straight line...

**6**

a long curve...

a long curve...

**7**

a crest...

a mouth...

a line...

a line...

three curved lines...

**8**

face markings...

an eye...

a neck pouch...

fur...

and four feet.

# How to draw an Agustinia (ag-us-tin-ee-a)

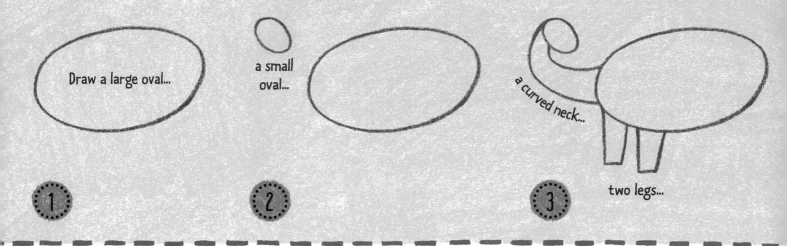

**1** Draw a large oval...

**2** a small oval...

**3** a curved neck...

two legs...

Your turn...

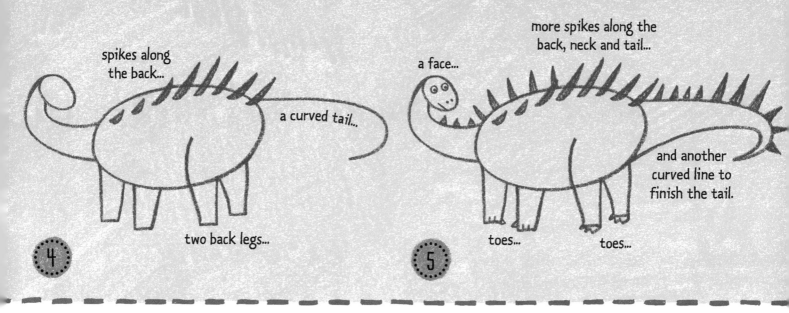

spikes along
the back...

a curved tail...

two back legs...

**4**

more spikes along the
back, neck and tail...

a face...

and another
curved line to
finish the tail.

toes...          toes...

**5**

# How to draw an Ichthyosaurus
(ik-thee-oh-sore-us)

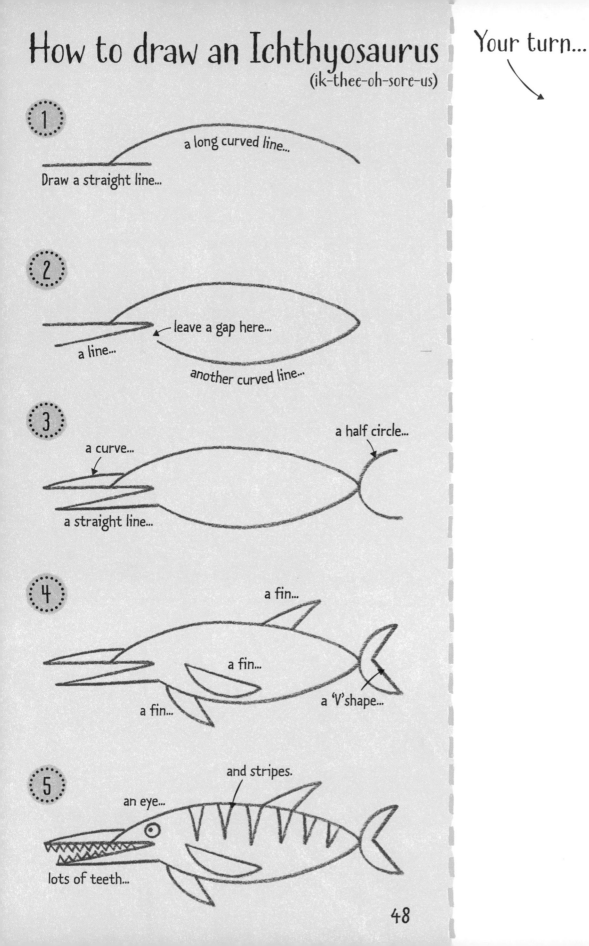

**1** Draw a straight line... a long curved line...

**2** a line... leave a gap here... another curved line...

**3** a curve... a straight line... a half circle...

**4** a fin... a fin... a fin... a 'V' shape...

**5** an eye... and stripes. lots of teeth...

48

# How to draw a Microraptor (my-crow-rap-tor)

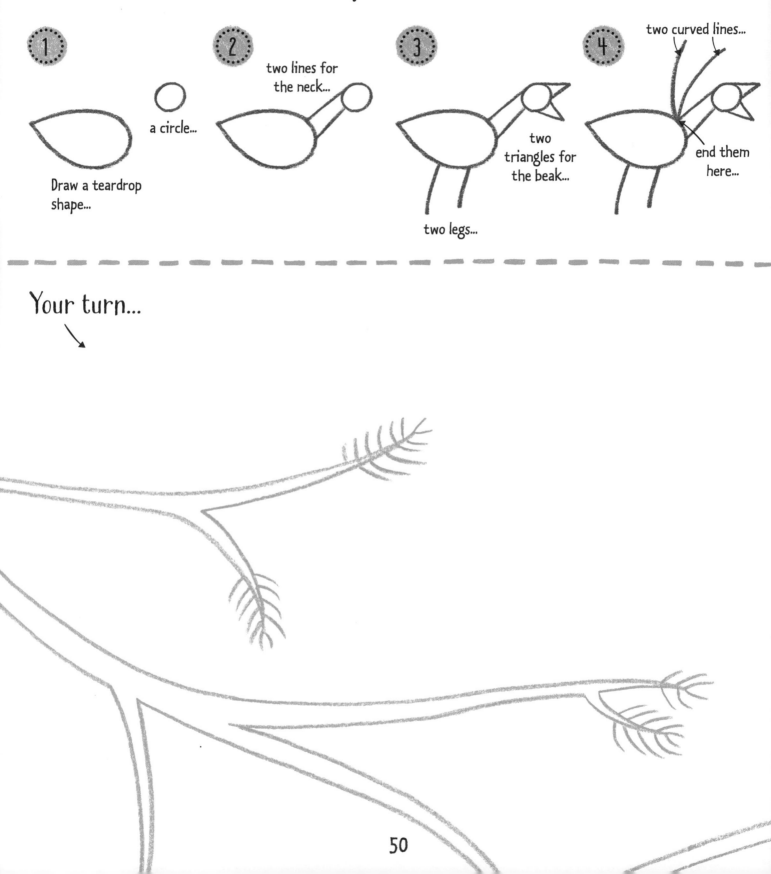

**1**

Draw a teardrop shape...

a circle...

**2**

two lines for the neck...

**3**

two triangles for the beak...

two legs...

**4**

two curved lines...

end them here...

Your turn...

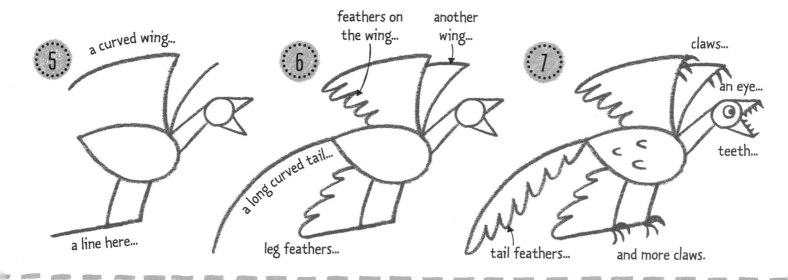

**5** a curved wing...

a line here...

**6** feathers on the wing... another wing...

a long curved tail...

leg feathers...

**7** claws...

an eye...

teeth...

tail feathers... and more claws.

# How to draw an Exaeretodon
(ex-air-ret-oh-don)

Your turn...

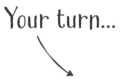

1. Draw a curved line... and a straight line...

2. a curve underneath...

3. a line...
   a short line...
   another line...

4. a curved tail...
   a C-shaped mouth...

5. four legs and feet...

6. fur...
   an ear, eye and nose...
   a sharp tooth...
   and whiskers.

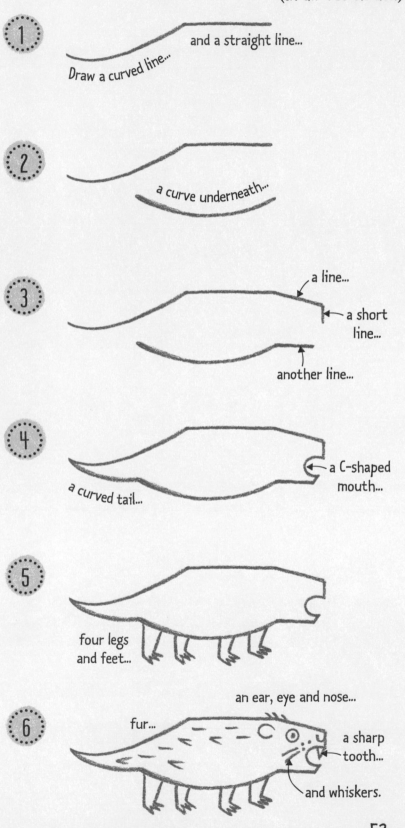

52

# How to draw an Archaeopteryx (ar-kee-op-tur-iks)

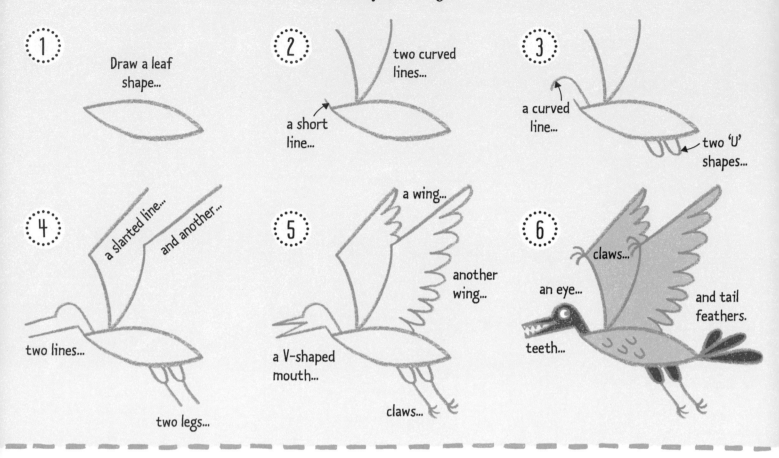

1. Draw a leaf shape...

2. a short line... two curved lines...

3. a curved line... two 'U' shapes...

4. a slanted line... and another... two lines... two legs...

5. a wing... another wing... a V-shaped mouth... claws...

6. claws... an eye... teeth... and tail feathers.

Your turn...

# How to draw a Mononykus (mon-non-i-kus)

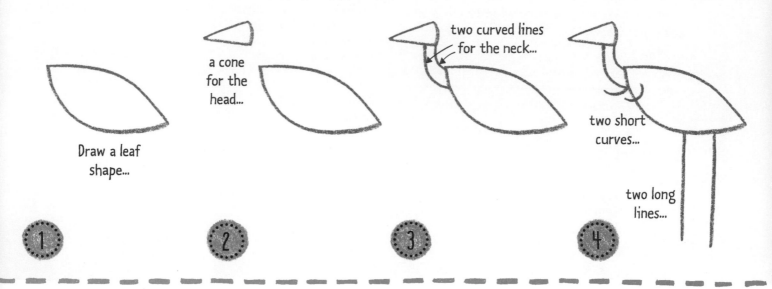

Draw a leaf shape...

a cone for the head...

two curved lines for the neck...

two short curves...

two long lines...

1

2

3

4

Your turn...

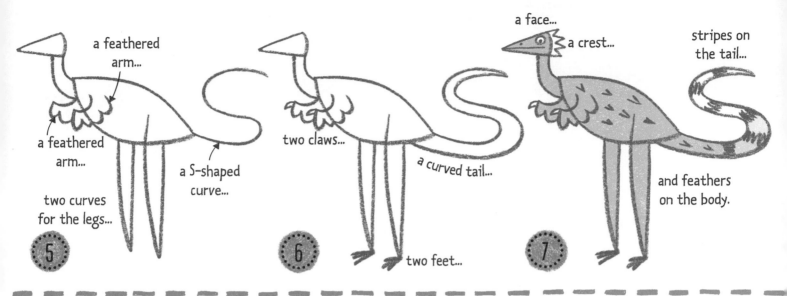

a feathered arm...

a feathered arm...

two curves for the legs...

a S-shaped curve...

**5**

two claws...

a curved tail...

two feet...

**6**

a face...

a crest...

stripes on the tail...

and feathers on the body.

**7**

# How to draw a Gigantoraptor

(jy-gant-oh-rap-tor)

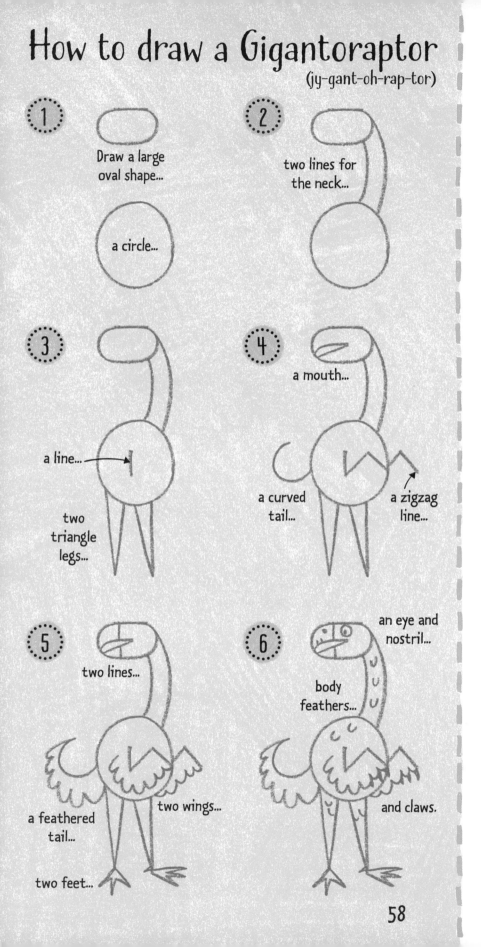

**1** Draw a large oval shape... a circle...

**2** two lines for the neck...

**3** a line... two triangle legs...

**4** a mouth... a curved tail... a zigzag line...

**5** two lines... a feathered tail... two wings... two feet...

**6** an eye and nostril... body feathers... and claws.

Your turn...

# How to draw a Parasaurolophus (pah-rah-sore-oh-lo-fus)

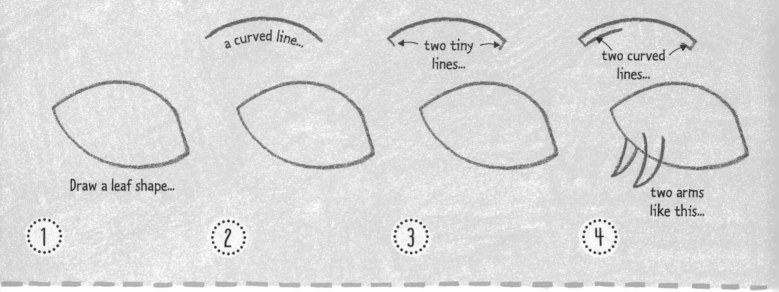

a curved line...

two tiny
lines...

two curved
lines...

Draw a leaf shape...

two arms
like this...

① ② ③ ④

Your turn...

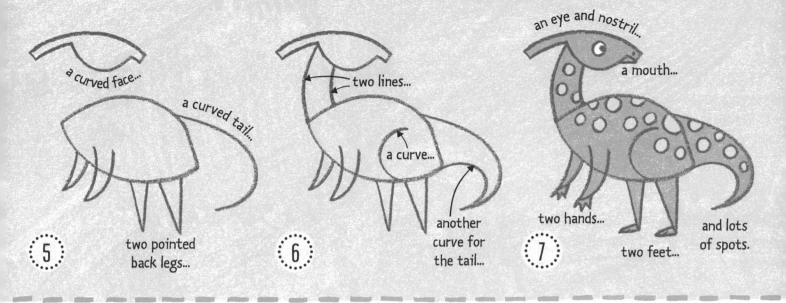

a curved face...

a curved tail...

(5) two pointed back legs...

two lines...

a curve...

another curve for the tail...

(6)

an eye and nostril...

a mouth...

(7) two hands...

two feet...

and lots of spots.

# How to draw a Velociraptor (veh-loss-i-rap-tor)

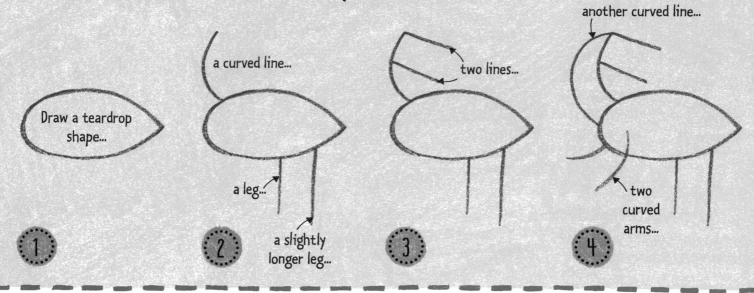

Draw a teardrop shape...

a curved line...

a leg...

a slightly longer leg...

two lines...

another curved line...

two curved arms...

1

2

3

4

Your turn...

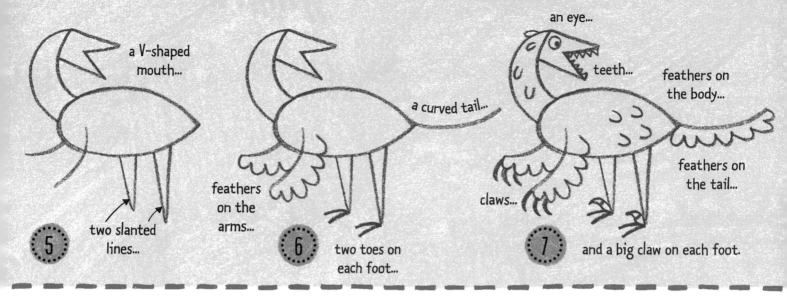

a V-shaped mouth...

**5** two slanted lines...

feathers on the arms...

a curved tail...

**6** two toes on each foot...

an eye...

teeth...

feathers on the body...

claws...

feathers on the tail...

**7** and a big claw on each foot.

# How to draw a Ceratosaurus (sir-rat-oh-sore-us)

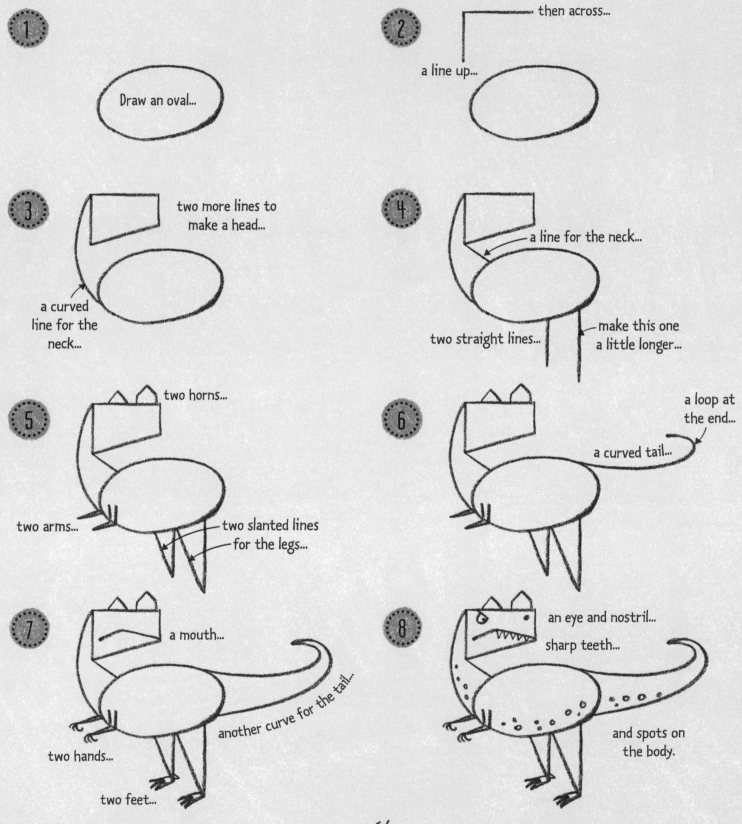

**1** Draw an oval...

**2** a line up... then across...

**3** two more lines to make a head... a curved line for the neck...

**4** a line for the neck... two straight lines... make this one a little longer...

**5** two horns... two arms... two slanted lines for the legs...

**6** a loop at the end... a curved tail...

**7** a mouth... another curve for the tail... two hands... two feet...

**8** an eye and nostril... sharp teeth... and spots on the body.

Your turn...

# How to draw a Stegosaurus
(steg-uh-sore-us)

1. Draw a leaf shape...
   a short line...
   a longer slanted line...

2. a wavy line for the back...
   a short line...
   a long line...

3. four legs...
   a curve for the tail...

4. lots of diamond-shaped plates...
   four spikes...
   a line...

5. a face...
   and spots.

Your turn...

66

Stegosaurus ate only plants, not other dinosaurs.

# How to draw an Anurognathus (an-you-rog-nah-thus)

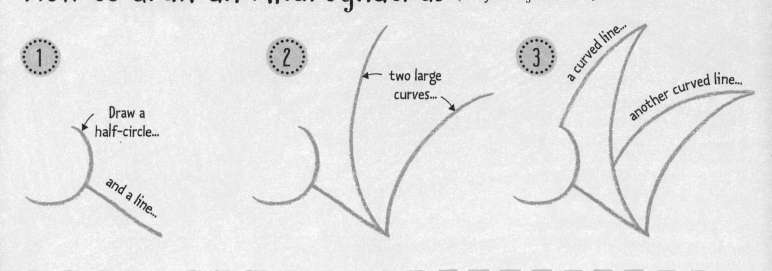

1 Draw a half-circle... and a line...

2 two large curves...

3 a curved line... another curved line...

Your turn...

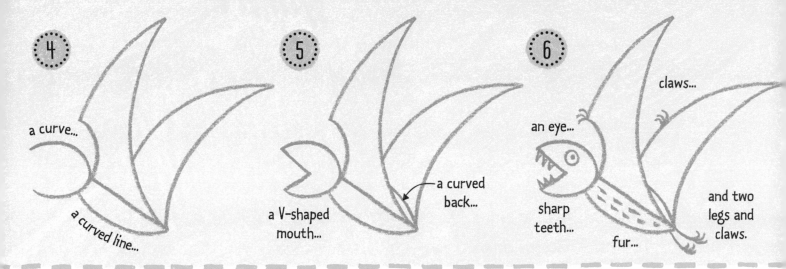

4  a curve...

a curved line...

5  a V-shaped mouth...

a curved back...

6  an eye...

sharp teeth...

fur...

claws...

and two legs and claws.

# How to draw a Triceratops (try-sera-tops)

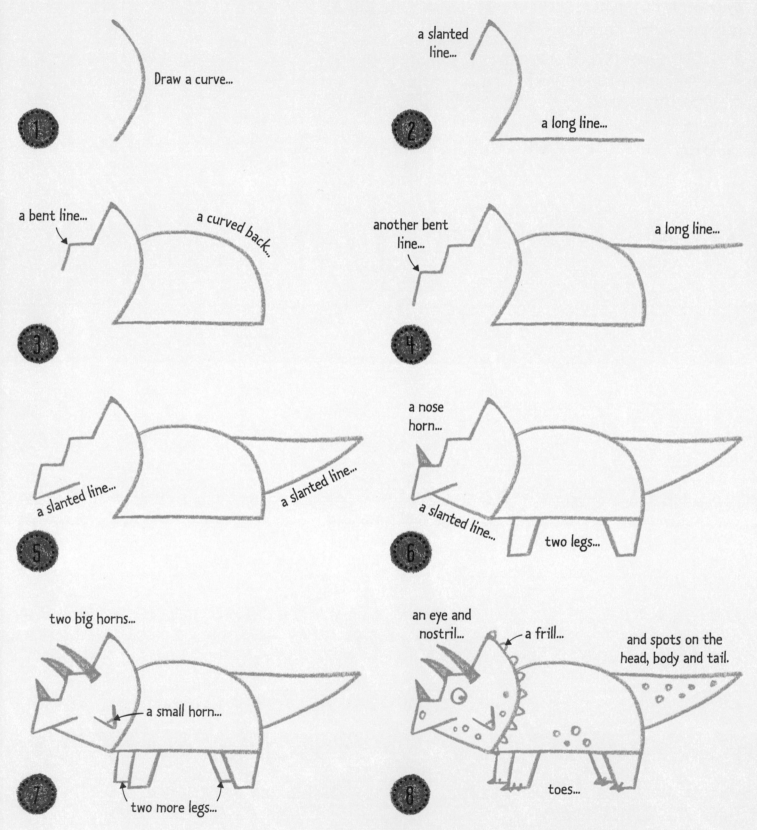

**1** Draw a curve...

**2** a slanted line... a long line...

**3** a bent line... a curved back...

**4** another bent line... a long line...

**5** a slanted line... a slanted line...

**6** a nose horn... a slanted line... two legs...

**7** two big horns... a small horn... two more legs...

**8** an eye and nostril... a frill... and spots on the head, body and tail. toes...

# Try this...

By drawing different heads on your Triceratops's body you can create lots of other similar types of dinosaurs. Here are some ideas that you could copy.

Einiosaurus

Torosaurus

Pachyrhinosaurus

# Your turn...

# How to draw a Brachiosaurus (brack-ee-oh-sore-us)

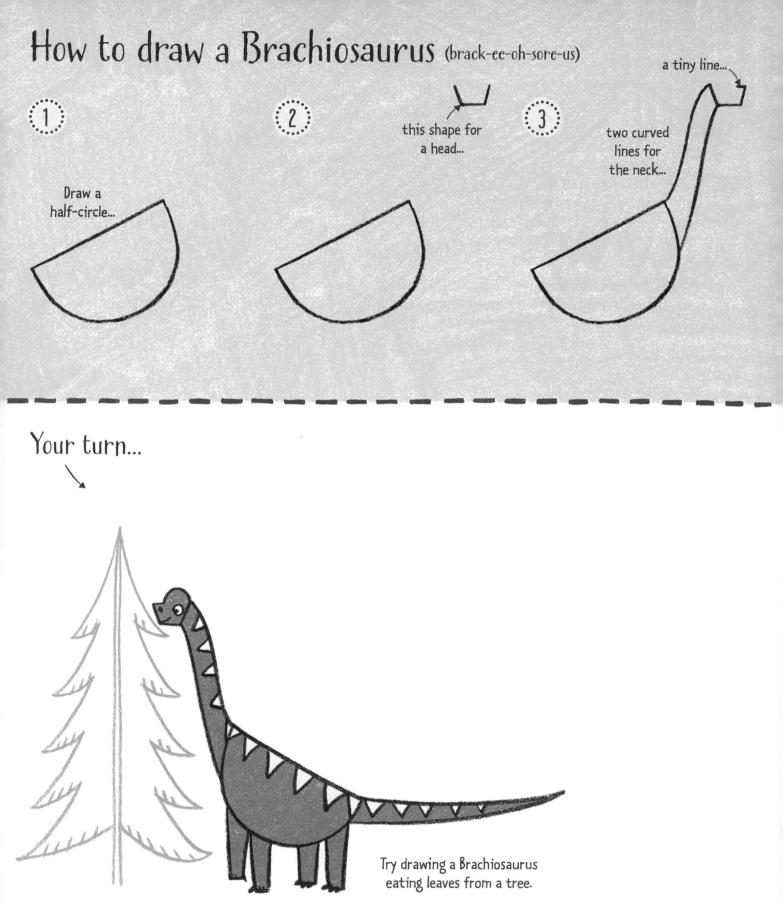

① Draw a half-circle...

this shape for a head...

② two curved lines for the neck...

③ a tiny line...

Your turn...

Try drawing a Brachiosaurus eating leaves from a tree.

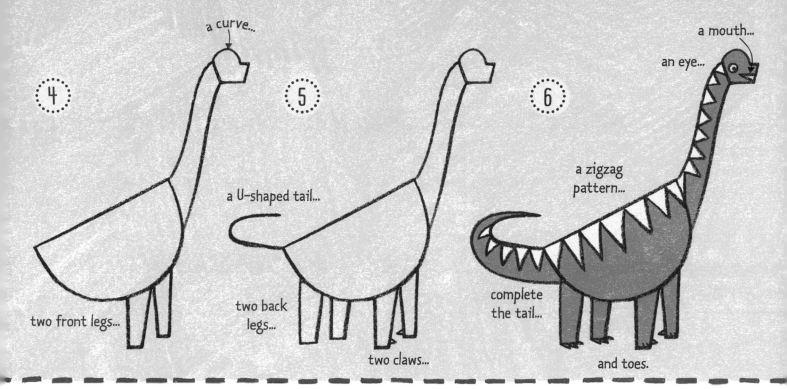

④

a curve...

two front legs...

⑤

a U-shaped tail...

two back legs...

two claws...

⑥

a mouth...

an eye...

a zigzag pattern...

complete the tail...

and toes.

73

# How to draw a Pachycephalosaurus (pack-ee-sef-al-loh-sore-us)

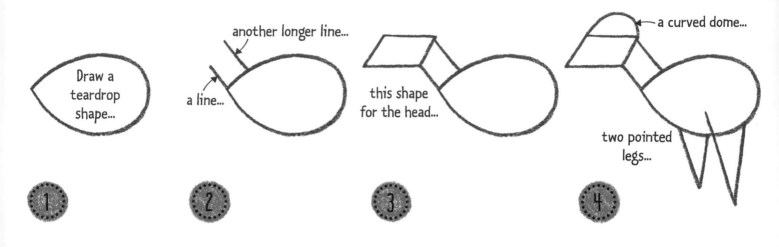

Draw a teardrop shape...

another longer line...

a line...

this shape for the head...

a curved dome...

two pointed legs...

1

2

3

4

Your turn...

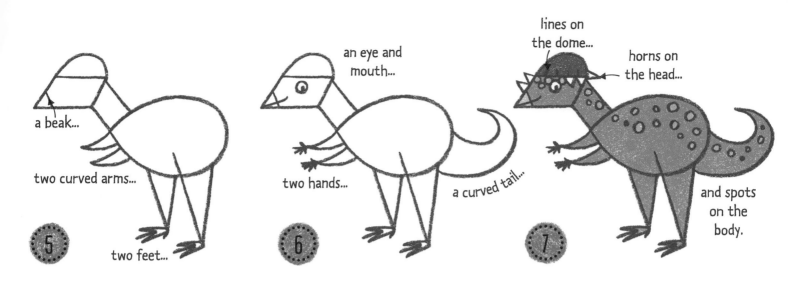

a beak...

two curved arms...

**5**

two feet...

an eye and mouth...

two hands...

a curved tail...

**6**

lines on the dome...

horns on the head...

**7**

and spots on the body.

75

# How to draw a Plesiosaurus (plees-ee-oh-sore-us)

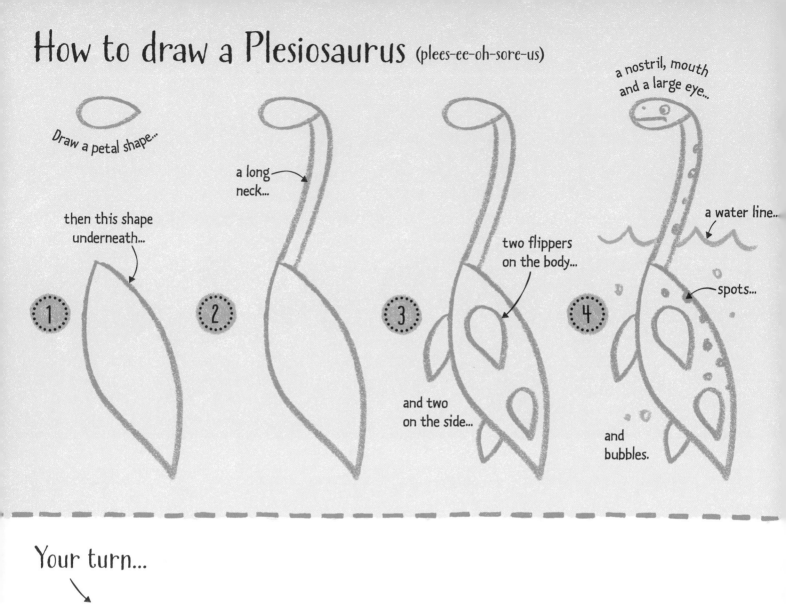

Draw a petal shape...

then this shape underneath...

① 

a long neck...

②

two flippers on the body...

and two on the side...

③

a nostril, mouth and a large eye...

a water line...

spots...

and bubbles.

④

---

Your turn...

# How to draw an Ischigualastia

(ish-ee-qual-as-tia)

1. Draw a curve... then a long straight line... a curve at the end...

2. extend the curve... a line...

3. a long curved back and tail... start here...

4. an oval mouth... four legs...

5. an eye and nostril... wrinkles... and the tops of legs. a snout... four feet...

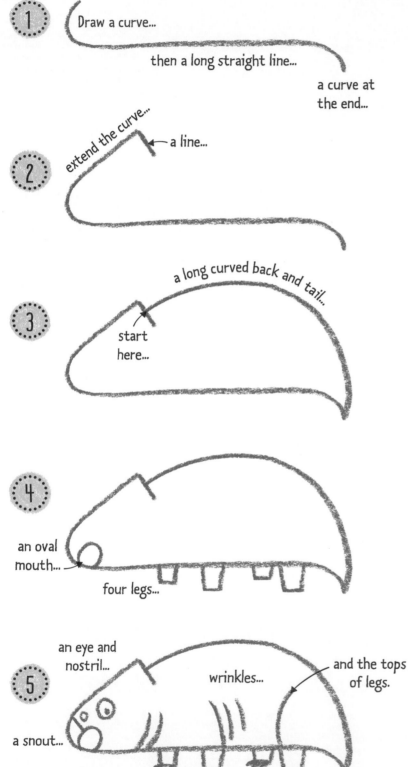

# How to draw an Ankylosaurus (an-kie-loh-sore-us)

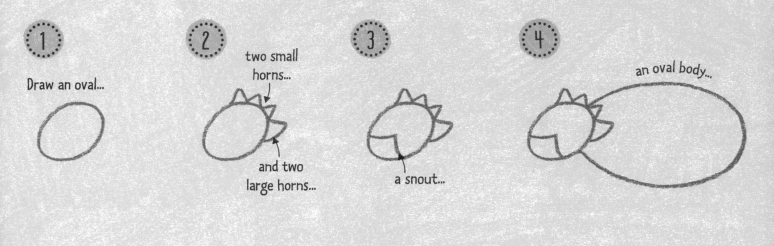

**1**

Draw an oval...

**2**

two small horns...

and two large horns...

**3**

a snout...

**4**

an oval body...

Your turn...

You could draw a straight tail like this...

**5**

four short legs...

**6**

a thick
curved tail...

**7**

and a
club tail.

bumps on the back...

a face...

toes...

# How to draw a hatching dinosaur egg

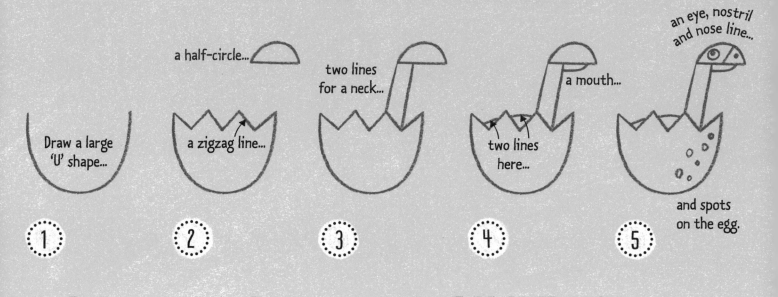

a half-circle...

Draw a large 'U' shape...

**1**

a zigzag line...

**2**

two lines for a neck...

**3**

a mouth...

two lines here...

**4**

an eye, nostril and nose line...

and spots on the egg.

**5**

Your turn...

# How to draw a volcano

Your turn...

① Draw a straight line...

② two slanted lines...

③ a zigzag...

④ two straight lines...

⑤ a curvy cloud...

⑥ lots of falling rocks...

and cracks

# How to draw a prehistoric tree

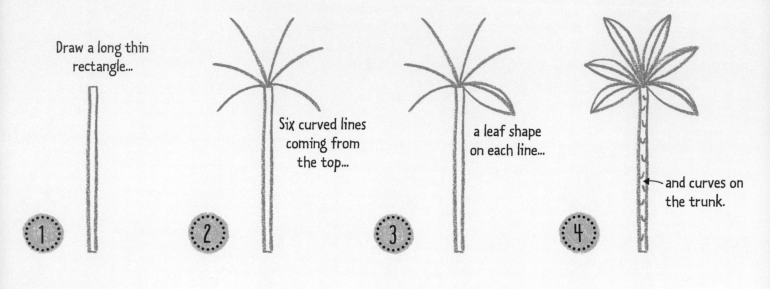

1 Draw a long thin rectangle...

2 Six curved lines coming from the top...

3 a leaf shape on each line...

4 and curves on the trunk.

Your turn...

# ...and another

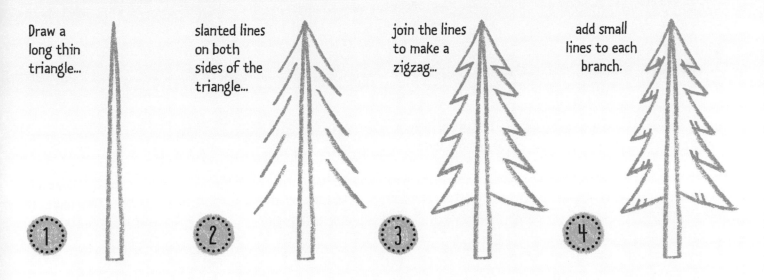

**1** Draw a long thin triangle...

**2** slanted lines on both sides of the triangle...

**3** join the lines to make a zigzag...

**4** add small lines to each branch.

## Try this...

Create different trees by changing the shape of the trunks and leaves. You could try different sizes too. Here are some ideas. You could copy them or invent some of your own.

fern-type leaves

a triangular trunk

a triangular trunk and wavy leaves

# How to draw a dinosaur skeleton

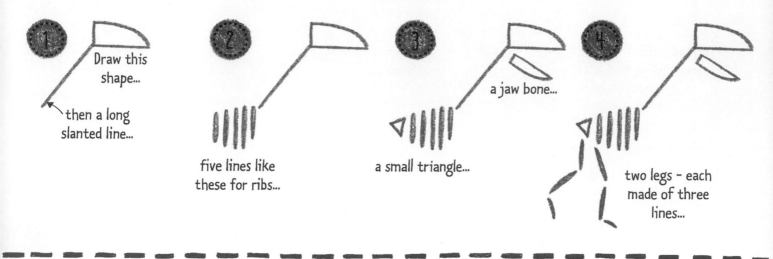

1 Draw this shape...

then a long slanted line...

2 five lines like these for ribs...

3 a small triangle...

a jaw bone...

4 two legs – each made of three lines...

Your turn...

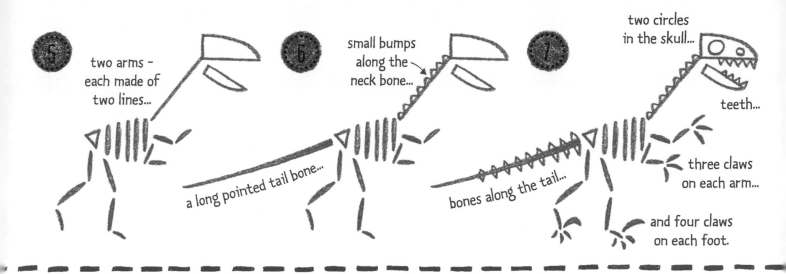

**5** two arms – each made of two lines...

a long pointed tail bone...

**6** small bumps along the neck bone...

**7** two circles in the skull...

teeth...

bones along the tail...

three claws on each arm...

and four claws on each foot.

# Jurassic scene

The following pages have ideas for scenes from different times when the dinosaurs roamed the land. Use the ideas from the other pages in the book to finish the scenes.

Draw another Stegosaurus looking out for danger.

Add Brachiosaurus eating this tree.

Add the spines to this Stegosaurus.

Add a baby Stegosaurus playing in the river.

Add more trees for a
Brachiosaurus to eat.

Draw a Ceratosaurus
looking for its lunch.

Add more leaves
for the Diplodocus
to eat.

# Cretaceous scene

Draw another erupting volcano.

Draw more footprints.

Add more rocks and ferns.

Draw another baby Triceratops.

Draw a big sun in the sky.

Copy this flying Quetzalcoatlus.

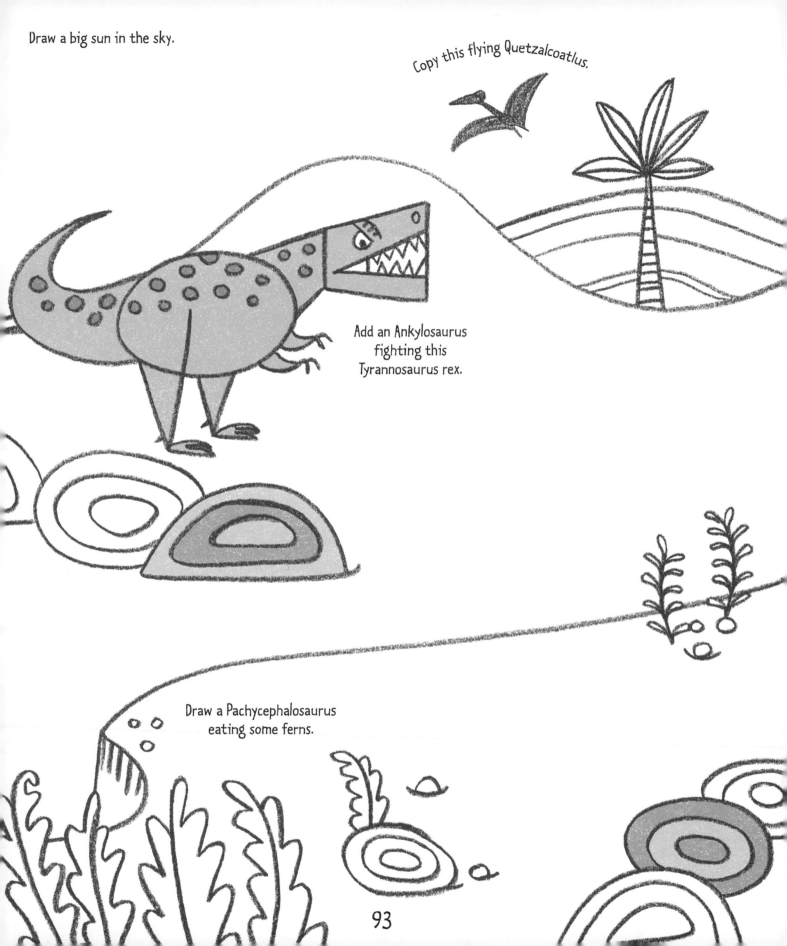

Add an Ankylosaurus
fighting this
Tyrannosaurus rex.

Draw a Pachycephalosaurus
eating some ferns.

# Under the sea

Draw more bubbles.

Draw another fish swimming away from the Rhomaleosaurus.

Add lots of sharp teeth in Rhomaleosaurus's mouth.

Draw lots more wiggly plants on the bottom of the sea.

Draw a Plesiosaurus with its head poking out of the water.

Add another Ichthyosaurus.

Copy this ammonite.

# In the air

Draw a flying Pterodactylus.

Add more eggs to the nest.

Add another Anurognathus.

Draw more fish in the water.

First published in 2016 by Usborne Publishing Limited, 83-85 Saffron Hill, London EC1N 8RT, United Kingdom. usborne.com